# Learn Programming
# With Flowcharts

Vijay Kumar Pandey

ISBN: 9798862777727

# DEDICATION

For those who love programming ........

# CONTENTS

# ACKNOWLEDGMENTS

I am extremely grateful to everyone who has contributed to the creation of this book, "Learn Programming with Flowcharts". Writing this book has been a journey full of challenges, inspiration, and growth, and it would not have been possible without the support and guidance of many individuals.

First and foremost, I would like to express my deep gratitude to my wife Jaya and my son Vishwesh. Her unwavering support, and patience, has been my greatest source of strength throughout this writing process. Your encouragement and belief in me has been my motivation to complete this book.

I am grateful to Dr. Brijesh Yadav and Dr. Shailendra Tiwari. Who have ignited my enthusiasm for this subject. Anand Mohan Pandey, Sujit Singh and Ashutosh Srivastava, thank you for sharing your expertise and insights, which have enriched the content of this book.

I am also thankful to our computer science department head, Dr. S.K. Singh, and our director in charge, Dr. Aman Gupta, for their continuous support and encouragement. Your guidance and belief in the importance of education have played a pivotal role in shaping this book.

To all of my colleagues, friends, and family members who provided valuable feedback and encouragement along the way, your contributions are greatly appreciated.

In the end, I heartily thank the readers of this book. Your interest in learning programming is what inspires writers like me to continue sharing the knowledge.

This book is the culmination of the collective efforts and support of these remarkable individuals, and I am truly grateful to each and every one of you.

# 1 SOMETHING ABOUT PROGRAMMING

## What is Programming?

*The process of writing a program is called programming.*

## What is a program?

*A program is a set of instructions to solve any given problem and to perform any particular task.*

We follow certain instructions to solve a given problem or to perform a task. The set of instructions is called a program. We also use it in performing various types of daily life activities. For example, when we wake up in the morning, we think about the activities of the day. Where to go today? Whom do you want to meet? What to talk about? We start working accordingly. At the same time, if there is any interruption, then we also make some changes in our program.

Along with the activities of daily life, programs are also used in many other areas, such as the basic operations of mathematics (addition, subtraction, multiplication, or division) with the help of the program itself. We perform the basic operations of mathematics based on the instructions we have already learned. A person who does not know about these basic operations of math will not be able to perform multiplication and division of two numbers because he does not have the knowledge of the instructions that enable addition, subtraction, multiplication, and division.

The main purpose of the program is to write the process of solving a problem in such a way that anyone can follow it and solve the problem easily, even if they do not know the solution to that problem beforehand. Suppose a person knows how to multiply two-digit numbers but does not know how to multiply three-digit numbers. If the same person is explained the method of multiplying three-digit numbers, then the person who could not multiply three-digit numbers before can now do it. Suppose a person does not know how to use an English dictionary, but when they are explained how to use the dictionary, then they can use it.

How to multiply a three-digit number or read a dictionary is just a program. A program is nothing but a method of doing a task. The only difference between a normal program and a computer program is that we humans only understand or explain the normal program, whereas the computer program is written with the help of any programming language. The main purpose of a general program is to make a person understand

3

the method of doing a task, whereas the main purpose of a computer program is to get some work done by the computer.

With the help of the program, we can solve any problem or learn new work. If we consider it, the meaning of learning is to incorporate a new program into ourselves. Like humans, programs are needed to get work done by a computer. Also, computers cannot do any work without a program, so it is inevitable to use a program to get new work done by a computer.

## What is Language?

Language serves as a medium of communication. With the help of language, two people or devices can effectively communicate. In other words, the means we employ to convey our messages to others is referred to as language.

Language can take various forms—it can be written, spoken, or conveyed through signs. It adapts to different situations and purposes, but its primary function is always to facilitate communication.

## Programming Language:

Now that we have understood the concepts of program, programming, and language, let's delve into programming languages.

Imagine you want to perform a task on a computer that it cannot do by itself because it lacks the necessary software. For example, let's say you want to create a drawing. To do this, you would look for an application program like MS Paint on the computer, as you cannot accomplish drawing tasks in a plain text editor like Notepad. Therefore, whenever we intend to use a computer for a specific task, we require a program. If such a program already exists, we can install and use it. However, if there's no available software for the task, we need to write a new program because all software is created using programs.

We've established that a program is essential for solving problems or undertaking new tasks. Without understanding the program, neither can we neither solve problems nor tackle new tasks. Similarly, without language, we cannot convey our thoughts to others.

Based on the above explanation, we can conclude that a program is crucial for problem-solving. So, if we want a computer to solve a problem, it must comprehend the program on which it can base its actions or solve new tasks. This raises the question of how to convey this program to the computer.

We know that language is the means by which we communicate our thoughts to others. Therefore, we need a language that can convey our program to the computer. Computers are machines and cannot understand human language, nor can humans understand computer language. Thus, there is a need for a bridge between the two—a technology that acts as an intermediary.

The primary function of a programming language is to translate the programs we write into a language that the computer can understand. Once the computer comprehends this language, it can execute new tasks and solve new problems based on the provided program. Every task we perform on a computer, whether it's using MS Word, creating art in a painting program, playing a game, managing an Excel spreadsheet, or using database management software, relies on various programs.

A programming language is a computer language employed by programmers to communicate human-designed instructions to the computer. In simpler terms, it is the language we use to instruct the computer. Programming languages are instrumental in software development.

# Program Development Life Cycle

Program is the basis of all types of work done by computer or human being.
A computer is identified only by its program because a computer does any work with the help of software and software is nothing but a collection of programs. Computer performs all types of work with the help of programs written on the computer. Therefore, it is very important to write the program correctly because if the program is wrong then you will not be able to achieve the purpose for which the program has been written, hence the usefulness of the computer and the efficiency of the computer is in a way based on the efficiency of the program. While we have come to know that all the work of a computer is done with the help of programs, from this it can easily be said that the computer itself does not do anything but the program gets that work done. We write programs so that the computer can solve that particular problem.

Thus, it is quite clear that the computer does any work only because of the program. Therefore, the more correct our program is, the more useful the computer will be for us, and hence it is very important for the program to be correct.

The main objective of the Program Development Life Cycle is to teach how to write programs step by step. Because if any work is done systematically then it is more effective and chances of mistakes are less. Because it is often seen that if we do any work in a systematic manner then that work is done correctly and we get maximum benefit from it.

For example, if someone has to build a house and he starts the work without any planning (planning of the house, management of materials, interior design, consultation with engineer, arrangement of laborers etc.), then understand how much trouble will happen. Will Here the house is just an example, planning before starting any project is called a systematic approach. The larger or more complex the project, the greater the need for a systematic approach.

PDLC is a systematic approach to developing computer programs. With its help it becomes very convenient to write programs. It is essentially used by large software development companies.

The program development life cycle includes five phases. Which are as follows.

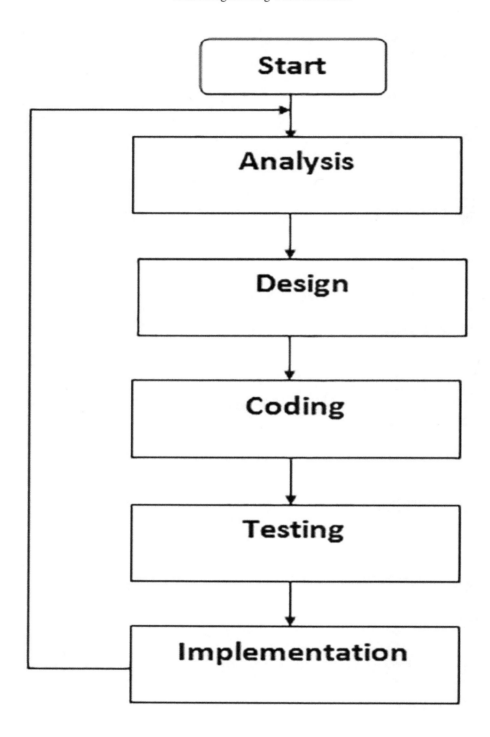

Program Development Life Cycle

# Analysis

This is the first stage of the program development life cycle. At this stage, we must have to know the clear and proper definition of the given problem. It is obvious that before going to solve the problem we must have to know about the problem itself. If we don't know about the problem how can we solve this? So before going to write a program to solve any specific problem or to perform any specific task we have to know a very clear definition of that.

Before doing any work, we must know what we have to do? Because if you do not know what to do, then you will not be able to do any work properly and if you don't know exactly what to do and start the work, then there will be more chances of it being wrong. If the program becomes wrong and later it comes in the wrong place, then both time and money are wasted. In order to avoid such wastage, it should be clear at the very beginning of the work what we want, even if the work starts a little late, but the work should be done in the right direction.

So it is very necessary to know about the problem itself before going to take any step towards the solution. Without knowing the problem or solving it with half-incomplete information, nothing will be gained except a waste of time. The success of the whole program was very much dependent on the analysis of the problem itself.

Suppose we want to make a program to print a table of two. To create a program, one must first know what a table is called. It means the complete definition of the table.

Without knowing about every detail of the table we cannot take further steps towards writing the program.

# Design

This is the second stage of the program development life cycle. It is also called the solution stage. After completing this stage we must have the solution to the given problem.

After clearing the definition of the problem, it is the turn that how to solve the problem? A programmer (a person who writes a program) finds a solution to a problem with the help of logic and his own experience and similar programs in the past. Logic has the most important role in solving any problem. The better the logic of the program, the more effective its program will be.

Basically to get the solution to the given problem is based on the ability of the programmer. There is no specific tool for getting the solution. Because of only the design stage, the involvement of human beings still exists in the field of computer science.

Logic representation tool

The logic of problem-solving arises mainly in the mind of the programmer because of his reasoning ability and skill.

We should not forget that our aim here is not to solve the problem but to solve the problem with the computer. So only the logic of problem-solving is not enough. After the solution to the problem is found, there is also a need for representation.

The main purpose of the Logic Representation Tool is to represent the logic of the programmer in the form so that any third person (even a computer) can solve the problem with the help of the logic used by the programmer.

## Algorithms

It is a logical representation tool.

An algorithm is a set of rules to be followed in a problem-solving operation.

The algorithm is a step-by-step demonstration of data processing or problem-solving.
Therefore an algorithm is a set of rules or instructions that define step by step how a task is to be performed in order to achieve the expected result.

This can be understood with the example of making a new recipe. When we make a new recipe, we go through the instructions and steps and execute them one by one in the given sequence. Algorithms designed are language-independent i.e. it is just simple instructions that can be implemented in any language

With the help of an algorithm, the programmer can explain his logic by writing it in a common language. With the help of this, any person who cannot solve the problem can solve the problem with the help of an algorithm. The aim is to explain the method to solve the problem. Directly or indirectly we use algorithms to solve any problem or to accomplish any task. The only difference is that we may have memorized the algorithm. We don't need to read it from anywhere. But many times it happens that when a new type of problem comes, then we look for its solution. Mostly the solution of a problem or how to do a task is explained only with the help of an algorithm.
This is the most used tool to represent logic because we do not need any special training or any extra effort to use it.
We simply write down the solution step by step.
While writing an algorithm, special care should be taken that it is being written for another person. So it should be very clear that there should not be any doubts.

## Flowchart

### *A flowchart is a graphical tool of problem-solving steps.*

## Common Flowcharts symbols

Different symbols are used for different types of instructions. And inside it, the instructions are written in brief. The direction of execution of the instruction is indicated by the symbol of the arrow. This makes the program very easy to explain and it is also easy to correct mistakes.

Many times the logic of the program is so complex that it is not convenient to represent it with the help of a common language.

**Flowchart symbols**

## *A Flowchart is a pictorial presentation tool of program logic.*

The standard symbol is used to create a flowchart. Any person in the world who makes a Flowchart or reads it can easily understand the meaning of those symbols. Hence Flowcharts made internationally are easier to create and understand.

With the help of a flowchart, it is easy to understand and explain the logic of the program. In fact, the purpose of writing a program is to explain your program to someone else. So whoever has prepared the solution of the program needs to know the flowchart. It is not that the logic of the program cannot be explained without a flowchart, but with the help of a Flowchart, even the most difficult logic can be explained in a very easy and effective way. It is rightly said that

A picture is worth a thousand words.

Sometimes a small diagram says many things instead of many words. That's why Flowcharts are considered a very effective tool for logic presentation.

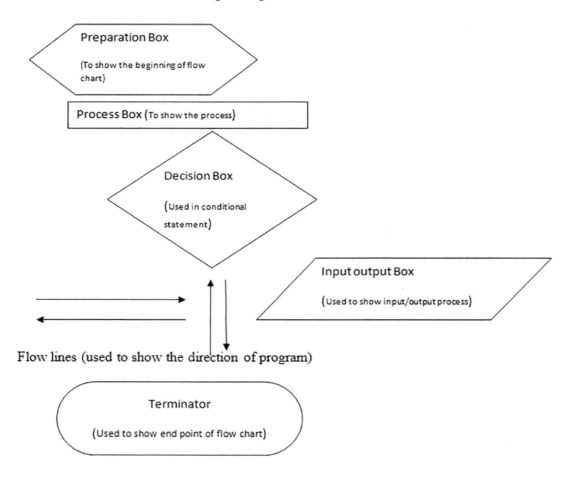

Some standard symbols used in Flowchart

## Coding

We can mainly divide the program development life cycle into two parts. Analysis and design come in the first part. In this part, we mainly analyze the problem and prepare the blueprint of the solution.
The main objective of the first step is to prepare a framework to solve the problem. The second part of PDLC works on the basis of this framework.

The second phase of PDLC is computer-based. The computer world starts from this phase.
If seen, any person who has the ability to solve the problem is useful for the first phase. But to work in the second phase, knowledge of computer language or programming language is necessary. As already discussed, the main purpose of language is to communicate its point of view to others. Here we mean to explain to the computer the blueprint or framework of the program created by the First Phase or the algorithm of the

solution. And to explain to the computer, we need some medium that can explain these things to him in his language.

In this stage, the algorithm or the content of the Flowchart is converted into a programming language and typed into the computer, which is called coding. Every programming language has its own coding style. Now as the name suggests (Language) and like every language, every programming language also has its own grammar, its own syntax, and its own keyboard. There are different types of programming languages for different situations for different types of different purposes. But the basic objective of all is the same, how to convert algorithms into computer language? Programming languages use compilers or interpreters to perform this task. With its help, the code written by the programmer is converted into machine language. Now the machine performs the process on the basis of the same code. In this way whatever algorithm was written at the design stage is converted into computer language. And we know that algorithms are written for a third person so that anyone can read the algorithm and solve the problem. Now that it is possible to convert algorithms into computer language, so the computer is also able to solve the problem for which the algorithm is written in ordinary language. There are many types of programming languages used in computer science Such as c, c++, java, HTML, python etc. After selecting the appropriate language, the algorithms in that language are changed and coding is done in the program.

The process of converting algorithms to a particular programming language is called coding. Each programming language has a different coding method.

For this, it is necessary for the person who is doing the coding work to have a good knowledge of that programming language.

The main purpose of coding is to convert the program into machine language. For this, a special type of program is used, which is called compiler/interpreter. With their help, the programs written by us in a high-level language are converted into low-level or machine-level language understandable by the computer. And on the basis of that, the computer solves the given problem, like a person after following the algorithm. An algorithm can do what it is written for, in the same way, a computer can do the same thing after coding very fast and without any mistakes. Because humans can make mistakes in following the steps of the algorithm, but the computer cannot.

Basically, the biggest advantage of a computer system is that the instructions are followed very fast and without any mistakes.

# Testing

Testing is a process to check whether a program behaves as desired or not, through actual execution. The program is executed and supplied with test data, and the way a program reacts to this test data is analyzed and the desired improvements are made to the program.

In this step, we check whether the algorithm or coding that is written and for which it is written serves the purpose. Simply put, checking whether our algorithmic flowchart or coding is correct or not is called testing because it is not sensible to implement the program directly without testing it. Therefore, first of all, programs, algorithms, logic, or coding are all tested first. There are various tools to test. It is a subject of computer science. Different types of tools like black-box testing, white box testing, etc. test the program with the help of a variety of techniques. If no defects are found in it then we proceed to the next step. But if any fault is found then it is removed, this process is called debugging.

The process of removing bugs is called debugging.

Many times computer programmers ignore this step but we must not forget that doing systematic work gets the job done properly and the basic purpose of the program development life cycle is to write the program systematically. And a systematic approach says that the program should be checked before direct implementation and this is actually a very wise move. For example, you've developed an algorithm that solves a problem, so before you tell that algorithm to the world, you'll want to test it out in different ways because if you once told someone and He will find fault in that. If he does so, you will be greatly insulted. So it is wise to test your algorithm first. Scientific people also make great use of testing. The success or failure of any experiment is decided on this level. Because sometimes it seems that our program or experiment was successful, but with the help of different types of equipment adopted in the test, we can find out the shortcomings which are usually not understood. For example, if someone makes a water ship and drops it directly into the water, then there is a problem in it, then the ship will sink and so much time, money, and labor will be wasted. Therefore the ship should be tested without being lowered into the water with the help of various tools, only after that it should be lowered into the water. This is an example, with the help of which we can understand the importance of testing.

## Implementation

In this stage, the purpose for which we write the program, that purpose is fulfilled. For example, if a person places an order for a company to get the software made of the bank, then the company uses all the stages of the program development life cycle. After the success of the testing stage, we can finally install that program or software by going to that bank so that now the bankers can use the software made by that company/person. Because their purpose was to make software for the bank and that purpose is not possible until the software is installed by going to the bank. Therefore, without the implementation stage, our entire program is meaningless. Therefore, this is the most final and most important stage of program development. Because the user does not have any meaning with the steps of writing our program or testing it or what problems he has seen in it, he only means with his program. The person who makes the final use of the program is called the end-user. The only thing that means to the end-user is whether the work we wanted to get done from the computer is now being done by the computer or not? The main purpose of making a computer program is to get that work done by the computer. Finally, it is seen whether that particular task is now being done by the computer or not, and if it is happening then it is installed in the computer. In the computer world, the implementation process is also called installation. This can be considered to be a shipwreck. Then what is the use of building a ship until the ship is not lowered into the water? Some people also associate the implementation stage with the maintenance state.

After some time after implementation, our system starts running. Our software starts running after some time requires maintenance. Because when the program is written, the situation at that time is different, after some time the time changes further. Changes come in many things. As there are changes in the bank interest rate, the fare in a train, bus, rail keeps on increasing, the tax rate keeps on changing. Therefore, the coding of the program also has to be changed. Or after some time some such problem comes which cannot be detected in testing, it is caught only when our software is installed. It is necessary to fix it after some time interval. This process is called maintenance. For this, the process is started again from the analysis state because whatever new problem has come up or whatever changes have to be made, it has to be understood again, then it has to be designed, then it has to be coding then it has to be tested and implement it in the last. Still some time passes, then the analysis is done, design is done, coding is done and after testing, it is implemented again. So this process goes on continuously as long as the software is used. That is why the term cycle is used along with program development because it is a continuous process that goes on again and again.

# Example:

To better understand the whole process of PDLC we can take the help of a problem i.e.

## Problem: how to print the table of a given number.

## Stage 1: ANALYSIS:

We know that at this stage we must have a clear definition of the given problem. We must have know what to do before how to do it?
After completing the analysis of the given problem we have the result ....
"Table writing is the process of multiplying the given number with one and showing the product. Again, multiply the given number by two and show the product. Multiply the given number with three and show the product. Repeat this process again and again until the multiplier reaches 10."

## Stage 2: Design

Finding the solution to the problem i.e. how to print the table of a given number?
Solution:
Algorithm
START

Step 1: Read the value of given number.
Step 2: Initialize i with 1.
Step 3: While i is less than 11, perform the step 4 otherwise go-to stop.
Step 4: Multiply the given number with i and show the product.
Increment i with one.
Go-to step 3

STOP

## Flowchart

Shows how to print the table of a given number.

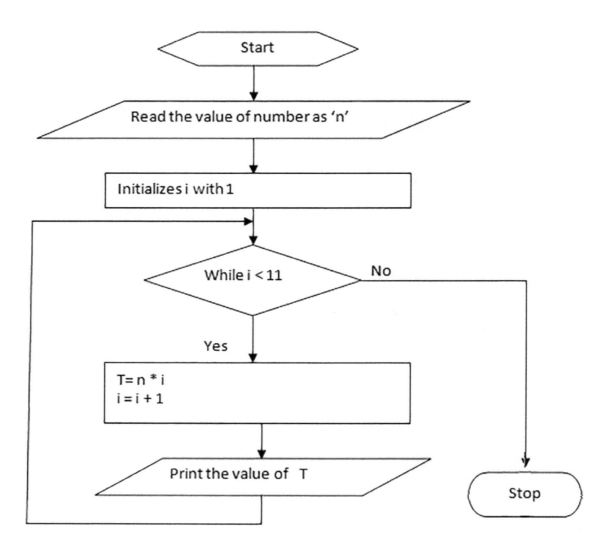

Flowchart for how to print the table of a given number

## Stage 3: Coding

A computer program in c language to print the table of a given number.

```c
#include < stdio.h >

int main()
{
int n, i = 1;

printf("Enter a number\n");
scanf("%d", &n);

printf("\nMultiplication table for %d is:\n\n", n);
while( i < 11 )
{
printf("%d x %d = %d\n", n, i, (n*i));
i = i + 1;
}

return 0;
}
```

## Stage 4: Testing

Let the value of n is 5


i = 1

T= n * i i = i + 1
i < 11 case true T= 5 * 1 i = 1 + 1
= 5 =2
i < 11 case true T= 5 * 2 i = 2 + 1
= 10 =3
i < 11 case true T= 5 * 3 i = 3 + 1
= 15 =4
i < 11 case true T= 5 * 4 i = 4 + 1
= 20 =5
i < 11 case true T= 5 * 5 i = 5 + 1
= 25 =6
i < 11 case true T= 5 * 6 i = 6 + 1

= 30 =7
i < 11 case true T= 5 * 7 i = 7 + 1
= 35 =8
i < 11 case true T= 5 * 8 i = 8 + 1
= 40 =9
i < 11 case true T= 5 * 9 i = 9 + 1
= 45 =10
i < 11 case true T= 5 * 10 i = 10 + 1
= 50 = 11
i < 11 case false

Program terminated

## Stage 5: Implementation

To implement this program install the program into the computer. And use it.

## Types of Programming Languages

The basic purpose of any programming language is to convert high-level language (humans can understand) into the machine-level language (computer can understand).

But one thing should also be remembered that every programming language has a specialized field.

Every programming language has a purpose. Keeping in mind the same purpose, any programming language is made. Today the field of computer is very wide. Today computer is used in the banking sector, in gaming, in telecommunication, in data processing, in railways, in airline reservation systems, in system designing, in face recognition, in voice recognition, in ATM machines, in aeronautics, in the entertainment industry, etc. If a computer is used to do any work, it means that that work will be done by some programs. Because we know that the computer does any work through the program itself. Therefore, different types of programs are also required to perform different types of tasks. Not all types of programs can be written by the same programming language. To write a particular kind of program, a particular kind of programming language is required. That's why there are many types of programming languages. Following are some of the main programming language types

**Markup Language**: HTML, XML, WML etc. are examples of some markup languages. A markup language is used to design the web page of the website. Whenever you go to a website, a page is present in front of you, that page is called a webpage. And the programming language used to create that page is called markup language.

**Scripting Languages:** Some scripting languages like JavaScript, VBScript, etc are examples of this. This is also related to the web page of the Internet. Where markup language is used to display the content on the web page, the same scripting language is used to perform some internal processing some logical activities in the web page.

We know that the Internet client is based on the server model. In this model, the client machine requests for a webpage or for any content from the server machine. This request reaches the server machine in electronic form using the network infrastructure. Now the server on the basis of this electronic request sends the appropriate content back to the client machine again using the same network infrastructure. In this way, the sequence of requests and replies goes on between the client and the server. It is to be noted here that a lot of network infrastructure is used in the process of this request and reply. Network infrastructure Capacity is limited, so it is necessary that the minimum use of network infrastructure is done so that the maximum number of people can use the Internet.

Such tasks related to some web pages that can be processed mainly on the local client's machine, which does not require a server, can be done with the help of scripting language. Suppose a student's mark sheet is to be viewed through the Internet, then the number of different subjects of that student's mark sheet will be stored in the server. Those numbers cannot be accessed without the help of the server but we do not need to reach the server to know the sum of all those subjects. This does not put unnecessary pressure on the server. There are many such tasks on the Internet that can be done on the local machine, they are called local processing. There is minimum pressure on the server on the Internet, there should be minimum load, and the emphasis is on maximum local processing to reduce the network traffic that does not unnecessarily request requests on the server. Programs related to local processing are created with the help of scripting languages.

**Server-Side Programming:** The Internet is based on the client-server model. We want to access it by typing the URL of a website from our computer's browser. This is a kind of request to the server. This request reaches the server. Now the server designs a web page based on the request received by the client and sends it to the client. The web pages to be developed based on the request of the client are called dynamic web pages. And with the help of server-side programming language dynamic pages are created. Examples of server-side programming languages are JSP, PHP, and ASP, etc.

**Systems Programming:** Some programming languages like c, c++ are used for system programming. Systems programming means creating programs that a computer system uses for itself. That does not interact with the user. This means that the user does not use this type of program directly. The user never knows when this type of program is used. Without these programs, our computer system cannot even function. As we know that there are two types of software, system software, and application software. Although application programs can also be created with the help of c, c++, they are specially used for systems programming, they are also called general-purpose programming languages. Various programs can be created with their help.

# 2 BASIC PROGRAM (SEQUENCE BASED)

In this chapter, we are going to learn some basic programs that are based solely on sequences. This means there is no need to use any conditional statements or iterative processes (loops).

Write an algorithm and draw the Flowchart for the following problems.

1. Draw a 10 meter straight line.
2. Draw a rectangle.
3. Interchange the value of two numbers (with third variable).
4. Interchange the value of two numbers (without third variable).
5. A man wants to bring a lion, a goat and grass across the river. The boat is small and can carry only one passenger at a time. If he leaves the lion and the goat alone together, the lion will eat the goat. If he leaves the goat and the grass alone together, the goat will eat the grass. How can he get all three across the river safely?
6. How to measure 1 litre of water using 5 litre and 3 litre cans?

# Solution:

**1. Draw a 10 meter straight line.**

**Algorithm**

Step 1: start with point A
Step 2: go 10 meter straight
Step 3: Stop drawing

**Flowchart**

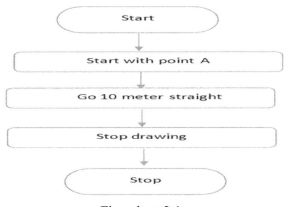

Flowchart 2.1

## 2. Draw a rectangle.

**Algorithm**

Step 1: Start with point A

Step 2: Go straight to the point B

Step 3: Turn right

Step 4: Go straight to the point C

Step 5: Turn right

Step 6: Go straight to the point D

Step 7: Turn right

Step 8: Go straight to the point A

Step 9: Stop drawing

**Flowchart**

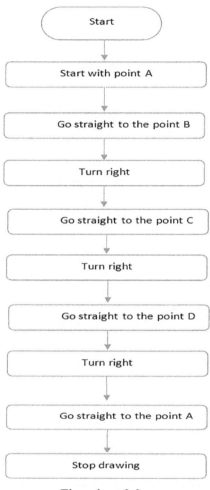

Flowchart 2.2

## 3. Interchange the value of two numbers (with third variable).

**Algorithm**

Step 1. Read the values of A and B.

Step 2. Initialize a third variable, name as "temp."

Step 3. Assign the value of A to temp: temp = A.

Step 4. Assign the value of B to A: A = B.

Step 5. Assign the value of temp (which was originally A) to B: B = temp.

Step 6. Display the new values of A and B after interchange.

Step 7. End of the algorithm.

**Flowchart**

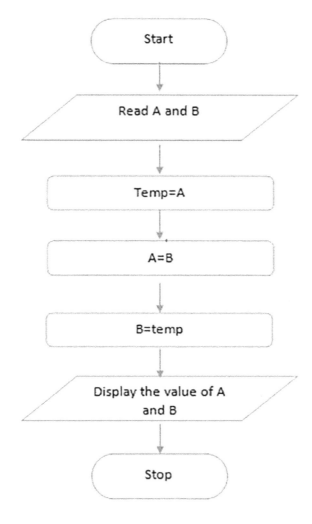

Flowchart 2.3

## 4. Interchange the value of two numbers (without third variable).

**Algorithm**

Step 1. Read the values of A and B.

Step2. A=A+B

Step 3. B=A-B

Step 4. A=A-B

Step5. Display the new values of A and B after interchange.

Step6. End of the algorithm.

**Flowchart**

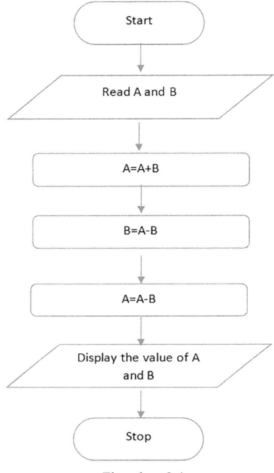

Flowchart 2.4

**5. A man wants to bring a lion, a goat and grass across the river. The boat is small and can carry only one passenger at a time. If he leaves the lion and the goat alone together, the lion will eat the goat. If he leaves the goat and the grass alone together, the goat will eat the grass. How can he get all three across the river safely?**

**Algorithm**

Step 1: Take the lion across the river and leave it on the other side.

Step 2: Go back alone to the initial side (left side).

Step 3. Take the goat across the river and leave it.

Step 4. Bring the lion back to the initial side (left side).

Step 5. Take the grass across the river and leave it.

Step 6. Go back alone to the initial side (left side).

Step 7. Take the lion across the river.

**Flowchart**

Flowchart 2.5


## 6. How to measure 1 litre of water using 5 litre and 3 litre cans?

**Algorithm:**

Step1:Fill 3 litre container

Step 2: pour it into 5 litre container

[ now5 litre container have 2 litre capacity, and 3 litre container have 3 litre capacity.]

Step 3: Fill 3 litre container again

Step 4: Pour it into 5 litre container till it is full

[nowthere is 1 litre water in 3 litre container.

**Flowchart**

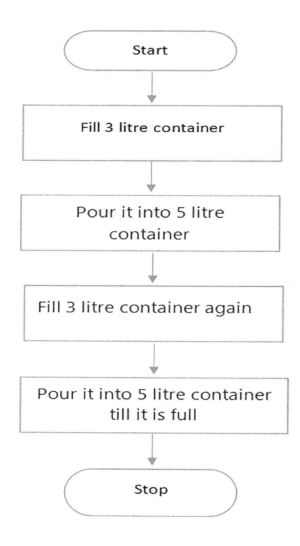

Flowchart 2.6

# 3 BASIC PROGRAM (SELECTION BASED)

Write an algorithm, draw Flowchart and write a program code in c language for the following problems.

1. To check whether a given Number is odd or even.
2. Find the greatest number between three numbers.
3. To check whether a given number is positive or negative
4. To check whether a given character is vowel or consonants.
5. To find whether a year is leap year or not.
6. To find division on the basis of total marks and total obtained marks are given by user.

## Solution:

Note : In many places you find a symbol '%' so first understand the meaning of this.

It is the symbol of mod in C language. It is used here for the purpose of simplicity, it is not mandatory. You can use the word 'mod' instead.

This returns the remainder.

Example:

x = 10
y = 3
r = x % y
Hence, if the value of r is divided by 10 by 3, the remainder will be 1.

r = 1

## 1. To check whether a given Number is odd or even.

### Algorithm:

Step1: Read the value of n.

Step2: if n is divisible by 2 then print "even"

       Else

       Print "odd"

Stop

### Flowchart

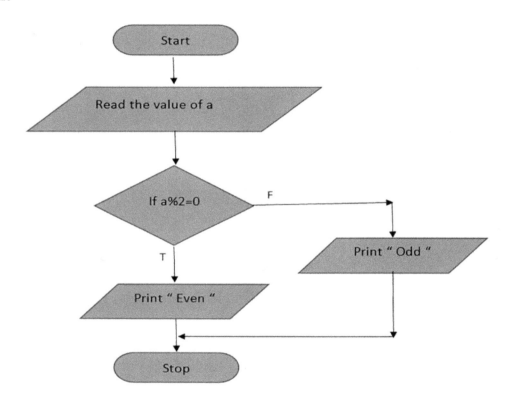

Flowchart 3.1

**C program code:**

```c
#include <stdio.h>

int main() {
int a;
printf("Enter a number: ");
scanf("%d", &a);

if (a % 2 == 0) {
printf("%d is even.\n", a);
} else {
printf("%d is odd.\n", a);
}

return 0;
}
```

## 2. Find the greatest number between three numbers.

**Algorithm:**

Step1: read the value of three numbers as a, b and c

Step2: check if a > b and also a > c then print "a is greatest number" and goto stop else goto
Step 3.

Step 3: check if b > a and also b > c then print "b is greatest number" and goto stop else goto step
4.

Step 4: check if c > a and also c > b then print "c is greatest number" and goto stop else goto
Stop.

Stop

**Flowchart**

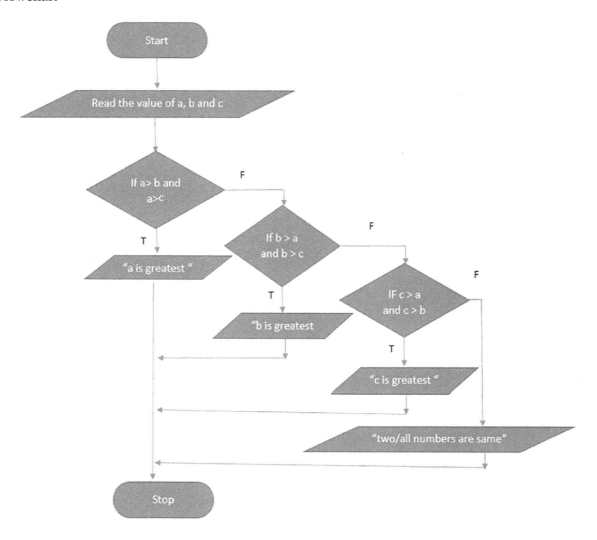

Flowchart 3.2

**C program code:**

```c
#include <stdio.h>

int main() {
float a, b, c;
printf("Enter three numbers: ");
scanf("%f %f %f", &a, &b, &c);

float max = a;
if (b > max) {
max = b;
}
if (c > max) {
max = c;
}

printf("The greatest number is %.2f.\n", max);

return 0;
}
```

**3. To check whether a given number is positive or negative.**

**Algorithm:**

Step1: read the value for given number as n.

Step2: check if n > 0 then print "positive"and goto stop else goto step 3.

Step 3: check if n < 0 then print "negative".

Stop.

**Flowchart**

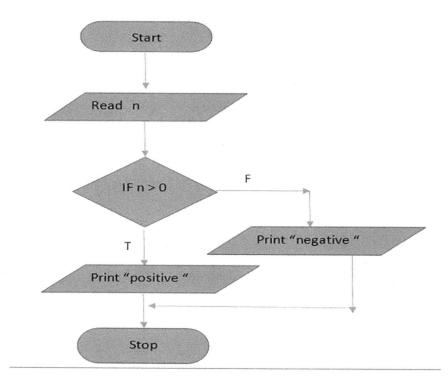

Flowchart 3.3

**C program code:**
```c
#include <stdio.h>

int main() {
float a;
printf("Enter a number: ");
scanf("%f", &a);
if (a > 0) {
printf("%.2f is positive.\n", a);
} else if (a < 0) {
printf("%.2f is negative.\n", a);
} else {
printf("%.2f is zero.\n", a);
}
return 0;
}
```

**4. To check whether a given character is vowel or consonants.**

**Algorithm:**

Step 1: Read the value for given character as ch.

Step2: Check if ch = 'a' OR ch = 'e' OR ch = 'I' OR ch = 'o' ch = 'u' then print "vowel "and go to stop else print "consonant ".

Stop.

**Flowchart**

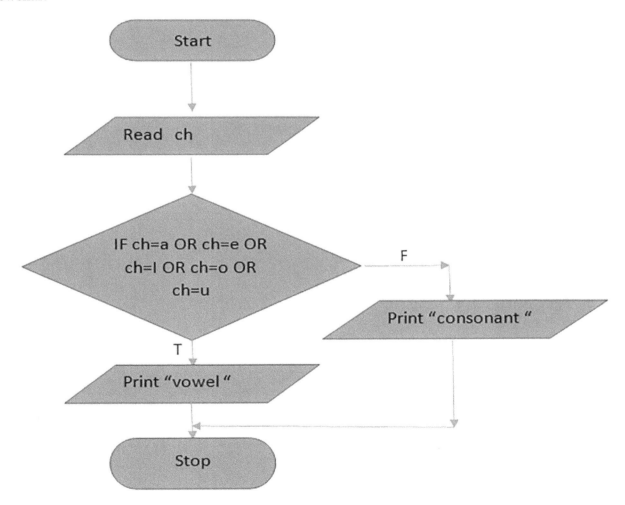

Flowchart 3.4

**C program code:**

```c
#include <stdio.h>

int main() {
char c;
printf("Enter a character: ");
scanf(" %c", &c);

if ((c >= 'a' && c <= 'z') || (c >= 'A' && c <= 'Z')) {
if (c == 'a' || c == 'e' || c == 'i' || c == 'o' || c == 'u' ||
c == 'A' || c == 'E' || c == 'I' || c == 'O' || c == 'U') {
printf("%c is a vowel.\n", c);
} else {
printf("%c is a consonant.\n", c);
}
} else {
printf("Invalid input: Not a character.\n");
}

return 0;
}
```

## 5. To find whether a year is leap year or not.

**Algorithm:**

Step 1: Read the value of year.

Step 2: If the year is divisible by 4, go to step 3. Else print "it's not a leap year".

Step 3: If the year is divisible by 100, go to step 4. Else print "it's a leap year".

Step 4: If the year is divisible by 400, print "it's a leap year". Else print "it's not a leap year".

Stop.

**Flowchart**

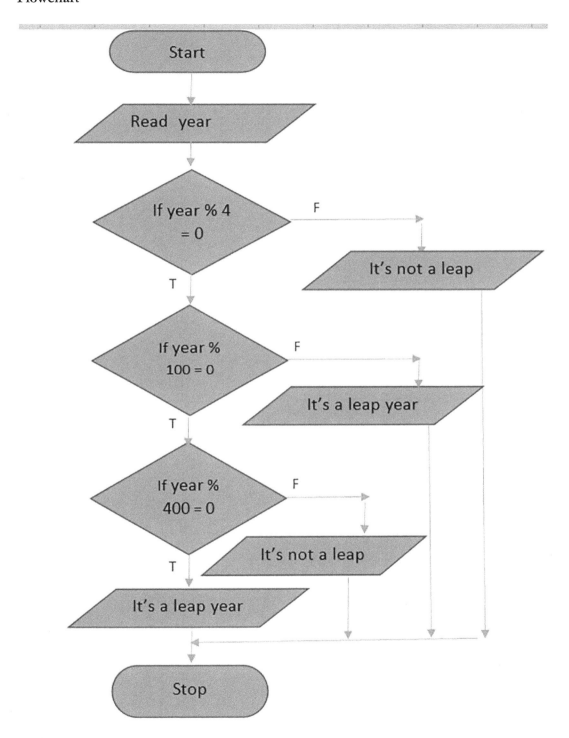

Flowchart 3.5

**C program code:**

```
#include <stdio.h>

int main() {
int year;
printf("Enter a year: ");
scanf("%d", &year);

if ((year % 4 == 0 && year % 100 != 0) || (year % 400 == 0)) {
printf("%d is a leap year.\n", year);
} else {
printf("%d is not a leap year.\n", year);
}

return 0;
}
```

**6. To find division on the basis of total marks and total obtained marks are given by user.**

**Algorithm:**

Step 1: Read the value of total marks and marks obtained as tm and mo.

Step 2: calculate per as mo /tm*100

Step 3: if per >=60 % print "First" and goto stop else goto next step.

Step 4: if per >=45% print "second" and goto stop else goto next step.

Step 5: if per >=33% print "Third" and goto stop else print"poor".

Stop.

**Flowchart**

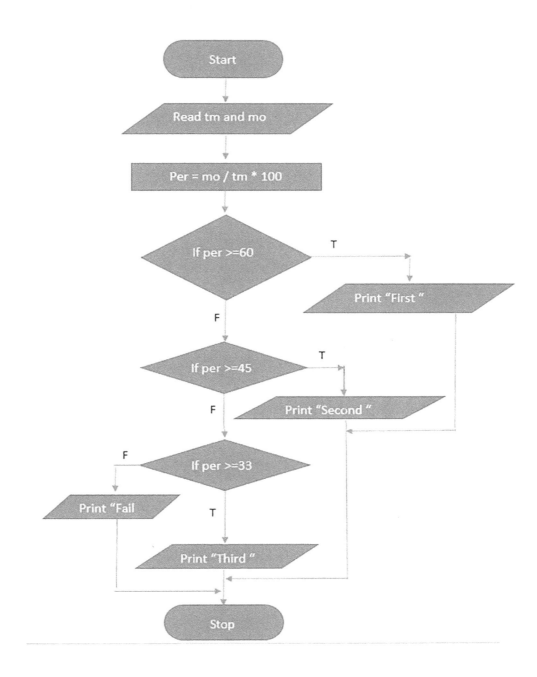

Flowchart 3.6

## C program code:

```c
#include <stdio.h>

int main() {
floattotal_marks, obtained_marks;
printf("Enter total marks: ");
scanf("%f", &total_marks);
printf("Enter obtained marks: ");
scanf("%f", &obtained_marks);

float percentage = (obtained_marks / total_marks) * 100;

if (percentage >= 80) {
printf("Distinction\n");
} else if (percentage >= 60) {
printf("First Division\n");
} else if (percentage >= 40) {
printf("Second Division\n");
} else {
printf("Fail\n");
}

return 0;
}
```

# 4 BASIC PROGRAM (ITERATION/LOOP BASED)

Write an algorithm, draw Flowchart and write a program code in c language for the following problems.

1. Find the factorial of a given number.
2. Check whether a given number is prime or not?
3. Print all prime numbers between two given numbers.
4. Print Fibonacci series.
5. Reverse the digits of a given number.
6. Sum of digits for the given number.
7. From 1 to 1000 sum of all numbers divisible by a given number.
8. Highest common factors of two given number.
9. Check whether a given number is perfect or not.
10. Check whether a given number is Ramanujan number.

# Solution:

**1. Find the factorial of a given number.**

**Algorithm:**

Step 1: read the value for given number as n. and

Step 2: result = 1

Step 3: If n is 0, set result to 1 and go to Step 6.

Step 4: Initialize i to 1.

Step 5: While i<= n, do the following:

Step 5a: Multiply result by i and update result.

Step 5b: Increment i by 1.

Step 5c: Repeat Steps 5a and 5b.

Step 6: Return result as the factorial of n.

Stop

**Flowchart:**

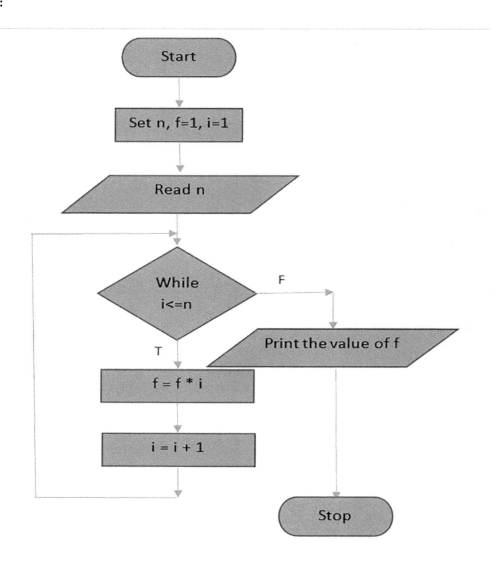

Flowchart 4.1

**C program code:**

```c
#include <stdio.h>
int main() {
int n, f = 1;
printf("Enter a non-negative integer: ");
scanf("%d", &n);
if (n < 0) {
printf("Factorial is not defined for negative numbers.\n");
} else {
for (inti = 1; i<= n; i++) {
f *= i;
}
printf("Factorial of %d is %d\n", n, f);
}
return 0;
}
```

**2. Check whether a given number is prime or not?**

**Algorithm:**

Step 1. Input a positive integer 'n'.

Step 2. If 'n' is less than 2, 'n' is not prime. Stop.

Step 3. Set 'isPrime' to true.

Step 4. For 'i' from 2 to 'n-1':

a. If 'n' is divisible by 'i':

- Set 'isPrime' to false.

- Exit the loop.

Step 5. If 'isPrime' is still true, 'n' is prime.

Step 6. If 'isPrime' is false, 'n' is not prime.

Stop

**Flowchart:**

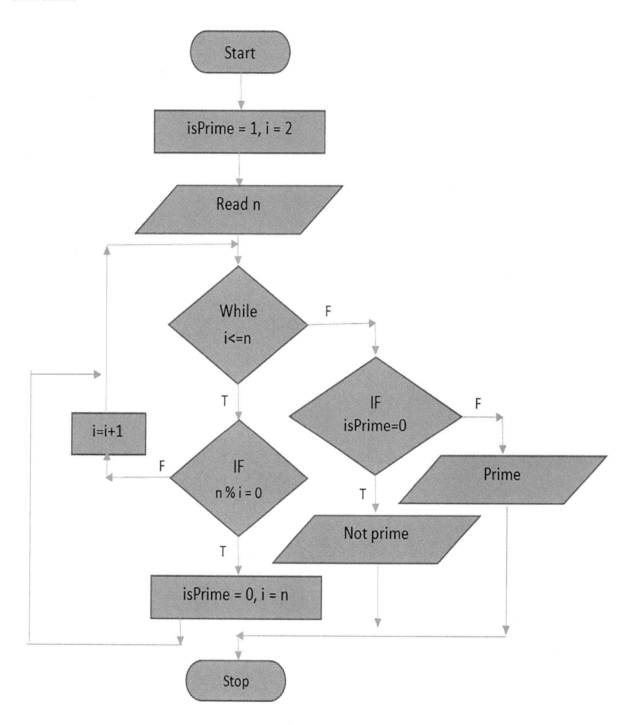

Flowchart 4.2

**C program code:**

```c
#include <stdio.h>
int main() {
int n;
intisPrime = 1; // We use 1 to represent true and 0 to represent false

printf("Enter a positive integer: ");
scanf("%d", &n);

if (n < 2) {
isPrime = 0; // 0 means false
} else {
for (inti = 2; i< n; i++) {
if (n % i == 0) {
isPrime = 0; // 0 means false
break;
}
}
}

if (isPrime==1) {
printf("%d is prime.\n", n);
} else {
printf("%d is not prime.\n", n);
}

return 0;
}
```

### 3. Print all prime numbers between two given numbers.

### Algorithm:

Step 1: Input two positive integers 'a' and 'b', where 'a' <= 'b'.

Step 2: Initialize 'n' to 'a'.

Step 3: If 'n' is less than 2, set 'n' to 2.

Step 4: Repeat the following steps for each 'n' from 'a' to 'b':

Step 4.1: Initialize 'isPrime' to true.

Step 4.2: For 'i' from 2 to 'n - 1':

Step 4.2.1: If 'n' is divisible by 'i', set 'isPrime' to false and break the loop.

Step 4.3: If 'isPrime' is true, print 'n' as a prime number.

Step 4.4: Increment 'n' by 1.

Step 5: End the program.

**Flowchart:**

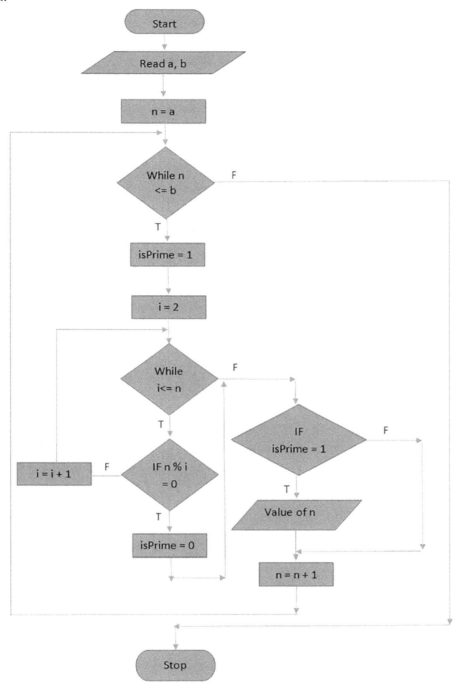

Flowchart 4.3

**C program code:**

```c
#include <stdio.h>

int main() {
int a, b;

printf("Enter two positive integers (a <= b): ");
scanf("%d %d", &a, &b);

if (a <= b) {
printf("Prime numbers between %d and %d are:\n", a, b);

for (int n = a; n <= b; n++) {
intisPrime = 1; // Assume 'n' is prime

if (n < 2) {
isPrime = 0; // 'n' less than 2 is not prime
} else {
for (inti = 2; i * i<= n; i++) {
if (n % i == 0) {
isPrime = 0; // 'n' is not prime
break;
}
}
}

if (isPrime) {
printf("%d\n", n);
}
}
```

```
} else {

printf("Invalid input: a should be less than or equal to b.\n");

}


return 0;

}
```

## 4. Print Fibonacci series.

### Algorithm:

Step 1: a = 0

Step 2: b = 1

Step 3: Input n

Step 4: Print a

Step 5: Print b

Step 6: For i = 2 to n:

c = a + b

Print c

a = b

b = c

Stop

**Flowchart**

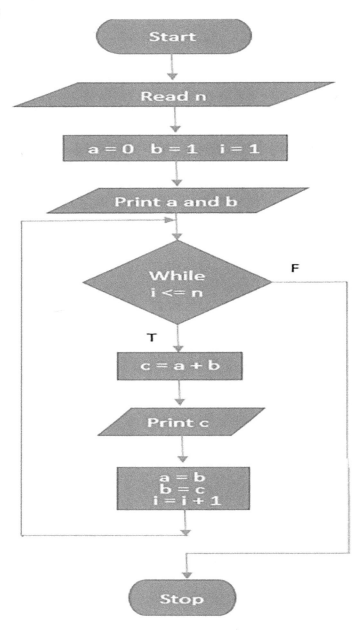

Flowchart 4.4

**C program code:**

```c
#include <stdio.h>

int main() {
int a = 0, b = 1, c;
int n;

printf("Enter the number of terms for the Fibonacci series: ");
scanf("%d", &n);

printf("Fibonacci series up to %d terms:\n", n);

if (n >= 1) {
printf("%d\n", a);
}
if (n >= 2) {
printf("%d\n", b);
}

for (int i = 3; i<= n; i++) {
c = a + b;
printf("%d\n", c);
a = b;
b = c;
}

return 0;
}
```

## 5. Reverse the digits of a given number.

### Algorithm:

Step 1: Input a positive integer 'n'.

Step 2: Initialize 'a' to 'n'.

Step 3: Initialize 'b' to 0.

     While 'a' > 0:

Step 4: Extract the last digit by 'digit' = 'a' % 10.

Step 5: Multiply 'b' by 10.

Step 6: Add 'digit' to 'b'.

Step 7: Divide 'a' by 10 (integer division).

Step 8: 'b' now contains the reversed number.

Step 9: Output 'b' as the result.

Stop

### Flowchart

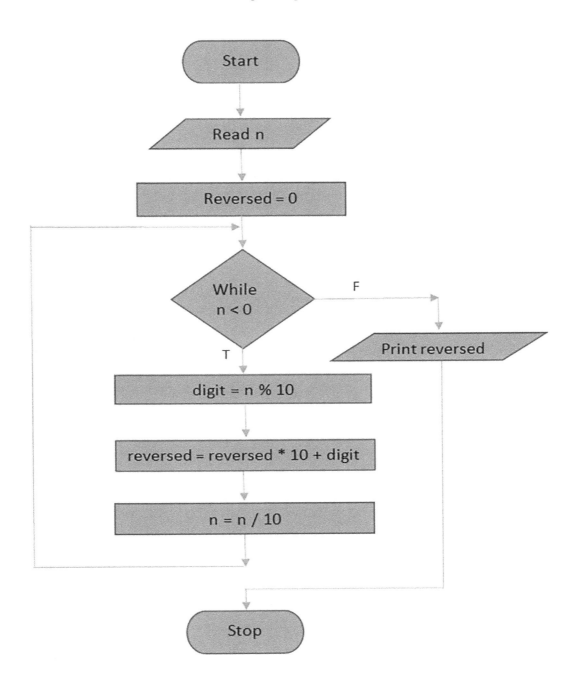

Flowchart 4.5

**C program code:**

```c
#include <stdio.h>

int main() {
int n, reversed = 0;

printf("Enter a number: ");
scanf("%d", &n);

while (n != 0) {
int digit = n % 10; // Get the last digit
reversed = reversed * 10 + digit; // Append the digit to the reversed number
n /= 10; // Remove the last digit from the original number
}

printf("Reversed number: %d\n");

return 0;
}
```

## 6. Sum of digits for the given number.

**Algorithm:**

Step 1: Start

Step 2: Initialize a variable a to 0

Step 3: Read the input number and store it in a variable b

Step 4: Repeat the following steps while b is greater than 0:

Step 4.1: Get the last digit of b by taking b modulo 10 and store it in variable c

Step 4.2: Add c to a

Step 4.3: Remove the last digit from b by integer division by 10

Step 5: Display the value of a as the sum of the digits

Step 6: End

**Flowchart:**

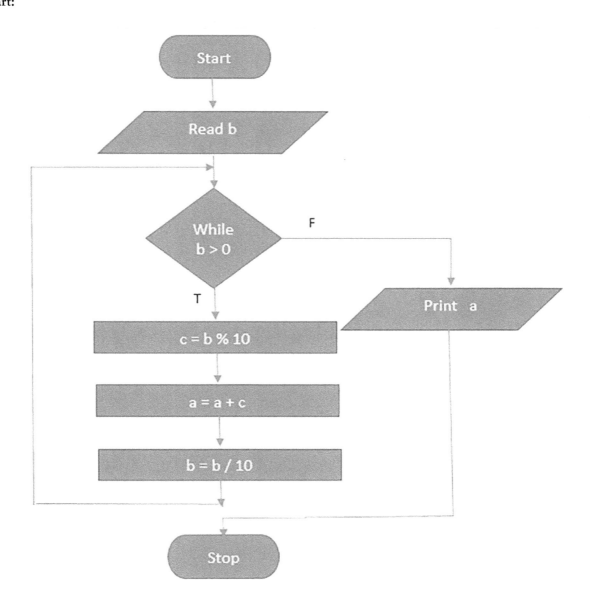

Flowchart 4.6

**C program code:**

```c
#include <stdio.h>

int main() {
int a = 0, b, c;

printf("Enter a number: ");
scanf("%d", &b);

while (b > 0) {
c = b % 10; // Get the last digit
a += c; // Add the last digit to the sum
b /= 10; // Remove the last digit from the number
}

printf("Sum of digits: %d\n", a);

return 0;
}
```

## 7. From 1 to 1000 sum of all numbers divisible by a given number.

**Algorithm:**

Step 1: Start

Step 2: Initialize a variable sum to 0

Step 3: Read the given number and store it in a variable n

Step 4: Repeat the following steps for each number i from 1 to 1000:

Step 4.1: If i is divisible by n (i % n == 0), then add i to sum

Step 5: Display the value of sum as the sum of numbers divisible by n from 1 to 1000

Step 6: End

**Flowchart:**

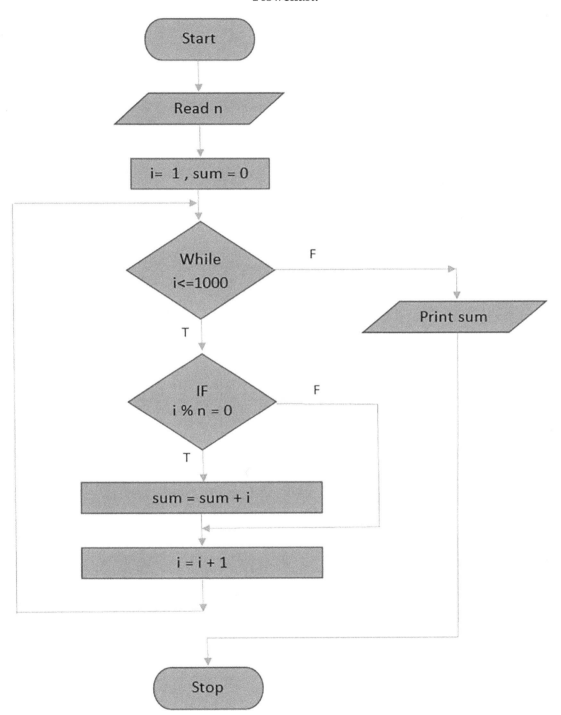

Flowchart 4.7

**C program code:**

```c
#include <stdio.h>

int main() {
int n, sum = 0;

printf("Enter a number: ");
scanf("%d", &n);

for (inti = 1; i<= 1000; i++) {
if (i % n == 0) {
sum += i;
}
}

printf("Sum of numbers divisible by %d from 1 to 1000: %d\n", n, sum);

return 0;
}
```

## 8. Highest common factors of two given number.

**Algorithm:**

Step 1. Start

Step 2. Read 'a' and 'b'

Step 3. Set 'hcf' to 1

Step 4. For 'i' from 2 to the minimum of 'a' and 'b':

Step 1. If both 'a' and 'b' are divisible by 'i':

Step 1. Set 'hcf' to 'i'

Step 5. Display 'hcf' as the highest common factor

Step 6. End

**Flowchart:**

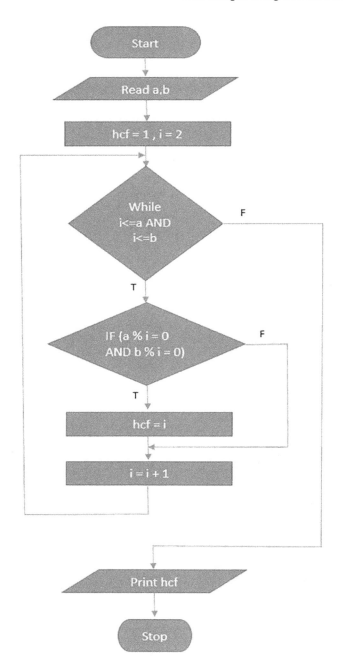

Flowchart 4.8

**C program code:**

```
#include <stdio.h>

int main() {
int a, b, hcf = 1;

printf("Enter two numbers: ");
scanf("%d %d", &a, &b);

for (inti = 2; i<= a &&i<= b; i++) {
if (a % i == 0 && b % i == 0) {
hcf = i;
}
}
printf("HCF of %d and %d is %d\n", a, b, hcf);
return 0;
}
```

## 9. Check whether a given number is perfect or not.

**Analysis :**

A perfect number is a positive integer that is equal to the sum of its proper divisors, excluding itself. In other words, a perfect number 'n' satisfies the following condition:

$$n = 1 + 2 + 3 + ... + (n-1)$$

In this equation, 'n' is the perfect number, and the sum on the right-hand side includes all positive divisors of 'n' except 'n' itself.

For example, the number 28 is a perfect number because its divisors are 1, 2, 4, 7, and 14, and:

$$28 = 1 + 2 + 4 + 7 + 14$$

**Algorithm :**

Step 1: Start

Step 2: Read the input number 'n'

Step 3: Initialize a variable 'sum' to 0

Step 4: Initialize a loop with a variable 'i' from 1 to 'n/2'

Step 5: While 'i' is less than 'n':

Step 5.1: If 'n' is divisible by 'i', add 'i' to 'sum'

Step 5.2: Increment 'i' by 1

Step 6: If 'sum' is equal to 'n', then 'n' is a perfect number

Step 7: Display the result (whether 'n' is a perfect number or not)

Step 8: End

**Flowchart:**

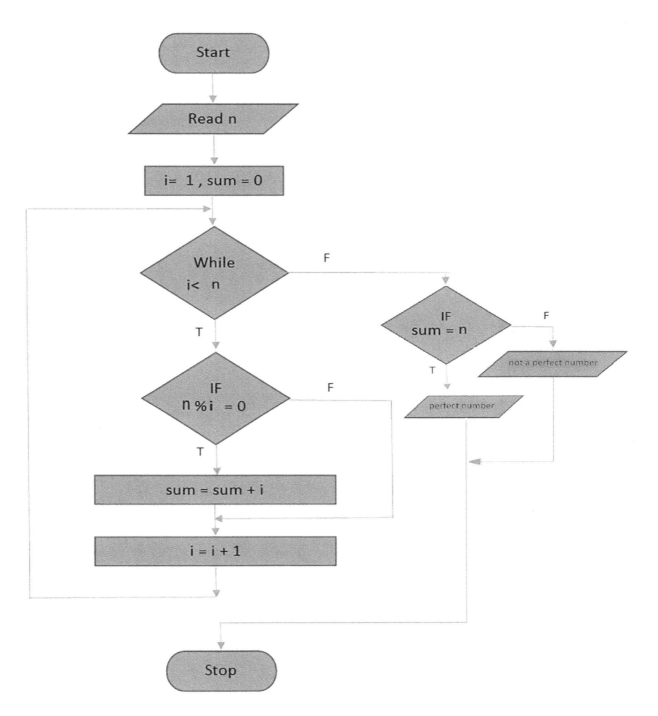

Flowchart 4.9

**C program code:**

```c
#include <stdio.h>

int main() {
intnum, sum = 0;

printf("Enter a number: ");
scanf("%d", &num);

for (inti = 1; i<num; i++) {
if (num % i == 0) {
sum += i;
}
}

if (sum == num) {
printf("%d is a perfect number.\n", num);
} else {
printf("%d is not a perfect number.\n", num);
}

return 0;
}
```

## 10. Check whether a given number is Ramanujan number.

### Analysis:

A Ramanujan number is a positive integer that can be expressed as the sum of two cubes in two different ways. In mathematical terms, a positive integer 'n' is considered a Ramanujan number if there exist four positive integers 'a1', 'b1', 'a2', and 'b2' such that:

$n = a1^3 + b1^3$
$n = a2^3 + b2^3$

The Indian mathematician SrinivasaRamanujan discovered that some numbers have this property, which is why they are named after him. Ramanujan numbers are a fascinating area of study in number theory and have applications in various mathematical and scientific contexts.

### Algorithm:

Step 1: Start

Step 2: Read the input number and store it in a variable 'n'

Step 3: Initialize a variable 'count' to 0

Step 4: Initialize a loop with a variable 'a' starting from 1

Step 5: While 'a' cubed is less than or equal to 'n':

Step 5.1: Initialize a loop with a variable 'b' starting from 'a + 1'

Step 5.2: While 'b' cubed is less than or equal to 'n':

Step 5.2.1: Calculate 'sum' as '$a^3 + b^3$'

Step 5.2.2: If 'sum' is equal to 'n', increment 'count' by 1

Step 5.2.3: Increment 'b' by 1

Step 5.3: Increment 'a' by 1

Step 6: If 'count' is greater than or equal to 2, then 'n' is a Ramanujan number

Step 7: Display the result (whether 'n' is a Ramanujan number or not)

Step 8: End

### Flowchart:

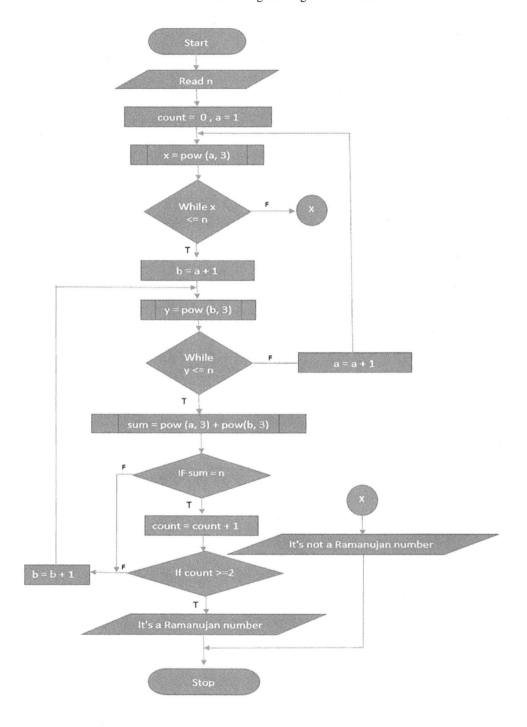

Flowchart 4.10

**C program code:**

```c
#include <stdio.h>
#include <math.h>

intisRamanujan(int n) {
int count = 0;
for (int a = 1; pow(a, 3) <= n; a++) {
for (int b = a + 1; pow(b, 3) <= n; b++) {
int sum = pow(a, 3) + pow(b, 3);
if (sum == n) {
count++;
if (count >= 2) {
return 1; // It's a Ramanujan number
}
}
}
}
return 0; // It's not a Ramanujan number
}
int main() {
int n;
printf("Enter a number: ");
scanf("%d", &n);

if (isRamanujan(n)) {
printf("%d is a Ramanujan number.\n", n);
} else {
printf("%d is not a Ramanujan number.\n", n);
}
return 0;
```

}

## Exercise : 1

Draw a flow chart for the following c code

```c
#include <stdio.h>

int main() {
int n, rn = 0;

// Input
printf("Enter a number: ");
scanf("%d", &n);

// Reverse the digits
while (n != 0) {
int d = n % 10;
rn = rn * 10 + d;
n /= 10;
}

// Output
printf("Reversed number: %d\n", rn);

return 0;
}
```

**Exercise : 2**

Draw a flow chart for the following c code

```
#include <stdio.h>
#include <math.h>

// Function to count the number of digits in a given number
int cd(int n) {
    int c = 0;
    while (n != 0) {
        n /= 10;
        c++;
    }
    return c;
}


// Function to check if a number is Armstrong
int am(int n) {
    int orig = n;
    int num_d = cd(n);
    int s = 0;

    while (n != 0) {
        int d = n % 10;
        s += pow(d, num_d);
        n /= 10;
    }

    return (s == orig);
}
```

```
int main() {
    int num;

    // Input
    printf("Enter a number: ");
    scanf("%d", &num);

    // Check if the number is Armstrong
    if (am(num)) {
        printf("%d is an Armstrong number.\n", num);
    } else {
        printf("%d is not an Armstrong number.\n", num);
    }

    return 0;
}
```

**Exercise : 3**

Draw a flow chart for the following c code

```
#include <stdio.h>

void printSeries(int n) {
    int num = 1;
    for (int i = 1; i <= n; i++) {
        printf("%d ", num);
        num = num * 10 + 1;
    }
    printf("\n");
```

```
}

int main() {
    int n;

    // Input
    printf("Enter the number of terms: ");
    scanf("%d", &n);

    // Print the series
    printf("Series: ");
    printSeries(n);

    return 0;
}
```

## Exercise : 4

Draw a flow chart for the following c code

```
#include <stdio.h>

int main() {
    int a, b = 0, c;

    // Input
    printf("Enter a number: ");
    scanf("%d", &a);

    // Save the original number
    c = a;

    // Reverse the digits
```

```
while (a != 0) {
    int d = a % 10;
    b = b * 10 + d;
    a /= 10;
}

// Check if it's a palindrome
if (c == b) {
    printf("%d is a palindrome.\n", c);
} else {
    printf("%d is not a palindrome.\n", c);
}

return 0;
}
```

**Exercise : 5**

Draw a flow chart for the following c code

```
#include <stdio.h>

int linearSearch(int a[], int n, int k) {
    for (int i = 0; i < n; i++) {
        if (a[i] == k) {
            return i;  // Return the index if key is found
        }
    }
    return -1;  // Return -1 if key is not found
}
```

```c
int main() {
    int n, k;

    // Input array size
    printf("Enter the size of the array: ");
    scanf("%d", &n);

    int arr[n];

    // Input array elements
    printf("Enter %d elements:\n", n);
    for (int i = 0; i < n; i++) {
        scanf("%d", &arr[i]);
    }

    // Input the element to be searched
    printf("Enter the element to search: ");
    scanf("%d", &k);

    // Perform linear search
    int r = linearSearch(arr, n, k);

    // Output the result
    if (r != -1) {
        printf("%d found at index %d.\n", k, r);
    } else {
        printf("%d not found in the array.\n", k);
    }

    return 0;
}
```

# ABOUT THE AUTHOR

The author has over 15 years of teaching experience in the field of computer science. He is an assistant professor at Rajarshi School of Management and Technology, U.P. College, Varanasi. He has guided numerous students in their software projects and delivered numerous guest lectures at many reputed institutes.

www.ingramcontent.com/pod-product-compliance
Lightning Source LLC
LaVergne TN
LVHW081803050326
832903LV00027B/2070